Phonics MONSTER

BOOK 3

i_e
igh

ai
ay
a_e

oa

o_e

ee
ea
e_e
ey

u_e
oo
ew

Long Vowels

Brian Giles

Joe Ruger

Table of Contents

Introduction

Phonics Monster - Book 3 offers a comprehensive introduction to the long vowels. This is an **"ESL Phonics"** book, which means that in addition to teaching the various sounds, it focuses on the differences between similar sounds which are especially difficult for ESL students (in contrast with native speakers, to whom such differences are natural).

Sections include:
- Word lists
- Practice sentences
- Rhyming words
- Games
- Reading practice
- Review quiz

Included in the final section is a longer reading passage to help reinforce all of the long vowels. The Appendix contains the answers to all of the quizzes and tests.

How to Use This Book

The book is divided into six sections: long a, long e, long i, long o, long u, and a review of all vowel sounds. When teaching each section, begin each lesson by reviewing the word lists and sentences.

Games

The Numbers Game – The Numbers Game consists of several numbered squares that contain a word from the section being taught. The game can be adapted to different formats:
- You, the teacher, call out a word, and the first person to yell out the corresponding number gets a point. The student with the most points is the winner. (The winner could then become the "tcacher," and call out words for the other students to find.)
- You, the teacher, call out a word. The first person to yell out the corresponding number then calls out a word for the other students. The first student to call out the number then calls out a number for the rest of the students to find, and so on. **(You may want to "eliminate" the students who have already called out a number, to prevent the same student from winning every time. For example, you can have every student stand up, and when a student correctly calls out the correct number, he or she can then sit down.)**
- Alternatively, you (or a student "teacher") can call out numbers, and the students can yell out the corresponding words.

Bingo – A blank BINGO gameboard is included in 3 of the lessons. Prior to playing, the students must write one word from the word list in that section in each of the squares. (This way, each student will have a unique gameboard.) The teacher then calls out words from the word list, and the students write an **X** over the word (if they have it on their gameboard). The first student to have five **X**'s in a row (vertically, diagonally, or horizontally) is the winner.

----

1. hail	same	day	ate
2. make	say	sake	rain
3. Jane	main	may	fake
4. ray	made	bait	mail
5. hate	mate	raise	cake
6. Gail	tame	gate	way
7. maize	nail	Fay	Kate
8. play	cane	make	fail
9. faze	Maine	vain	Gabe
10. gain	game	pail	bay

Long a – (ai, ay, a_e, ai_e)

1. Fay and Jane play on the same day.

2. Gail made a fake cake.

3. It may rain cats and dogs today.

4. Jed cut the cake and ate the cake.

5. Jay and Ray hate the name game.

6. Dave made a cake for Jane's sake.

7. Kate's mate hates the rain.

8. Dave can rake hay and play in the rain.

9. May Jake play the maze game?

10. Fay ate cake at the bay with Gabe.

Long a – ay vs. ai

You write **ay** at the <u>**end**</u> of a word:

- **b<u>ay</u>   d<u>ay</u>   h<u>ay</u>   J<u>ay</u>   l<u>ay</u>   m<u>ay</u>   p<u>ay</u>   s<u>ay</u>   w<u>ay</u>**

You write **ai** in the <u>**middle**</u> of a word:

- **b<u>ai</u>t   f<u>ai</u>l   g<u>ai</u>n   h<u>ai</u>l   l<u>ai</u>n   m<u>ai</u>n   n<u>ai</u>l   p<u>ai</u>n**

Write **ai** or **ay** in the blanks below; then read the words.

b___   b___t   s___l

r___se   l___   w___t

w___   w___n   d___

pl___n   pl___   m___l

y___   s___   p___n

j___l   l___n   m___

Long a – Rhyming Words

Rhyming words have the same **middle** and **end** sounds.
Some rhyming words look different, but they are rhyming words
because they **sound the same**:

- **bait** and **mate** are rhyming words
- **raise** and **maze** are rhyming words
- **lain** and **mane** are rhyming words

These are **rhyming words** because they have the <u>same middle and end sounds</u>.

*Remember: Listen to the sound; don't just look at the letters.

Look at the pairs of words below. Write yes (Y) if the words rhyme.
Write no (N) if the words do not rhyme.

1. make – take _____	7. day – may _____
2. bane – main _____	8. lane – pain _____
3. bake – tame _____	9. fate – fame _____
4. rail – sale _____	10. same – sake _____
5. bay – gate _____	11. gaze – maze _____

Short and Long a

Read the rows across. Listen for the difference between the **short a** sound and the **long a** sound:

hat / hate	Dan / Dane
bat / bait	fat / fate
lack / lake	sack / sake
sat / sate	pad / paid
tack / take	ran / rain
gab / Gabe	pan / pain
ban / bane	can / cane
tap / tape	Jan / Jane
razz / raise	man / mane
cap / cape	Bal / bale

Short a and Long a
Sentences

1. Can Gabe tape his cap to his cape?

2. Dan will ban tacks for the sake of pain.

3. Maine has rain, but lacks a lake.

4. Dan will tap the cane with his hat.

5. We sat at the lake in the rain.

6. The mad man hates the ban on tacks.

7. Dad's job is to raise the gate.

8. Pack the bag and take the bait.

9. The rain will make Jack late today.

Short a – Long a – Short e

These sounds can be very hard to tell apart. Practice reading across, and try to hear the different sounds.

	Short a	Long a	Short e
1.	man	mane	men
2.	fad	fade	fed
3.	tax	takes	tex
4.	bad	bade	bed
5.	pal	pale	pell
6.	sat	sate	set
7.	fat	fate	fet
8.	van	vane	ven
9.	Jan	Jane	Jen
10.	pan	pain	pen

Short a – Long a – Short e

Sentences

1. The med fad will fade.

2. The cat sat on the red pail.

3. Matt made a pen.

4. The fat vet takes tax.

5. Jen can make a man's bed today.

6. Dan is vain and Jen is sad.

7. Jen is a bad mate.

8. I met the lad Jade.

9. Jen's pen met the same fate as Jack's hat.

10. Matt's leg pain is bad.

Long a and Short a – Rhyming Words

Draw lines to match the rhyming words below.

bake	sale
tap	say
mail	take
day	lag
same	rap
bag	gait
pain	mane
mate	dame
ray	fad
sad	Kay

Review Quiz

Write the words and sentences that your teacher says on the blanks below. (Answer key in the back of the book.)

Part 1 – Words (6 points each)

1. _____   6. _____

2. _____   7. _____

3. _____   8. _____

4. _____   9. _____

5. _____   10. _____

Part 2 – Sentences (20 points each)

1. _____.

2. _____.

*See page 51 for more 'long a' reading practice.

1. feed	meat	Pete	key
2. thief	seek	team	meme
3. monkey	jeep	read	veal
4. he	bean	see	need
5. these	bee	heal	Eve
6. beam	keep	leap	we
7. brief	wean	fee	deal
8. pea	seed	eat	Steve
9. reek	seal	neat	deem
10. seen	Zeke	peel	keen

Long e

Sentences

1. We feed three monkeys.

2. We need to see the team.

3. Steve and Pete will not eat red meat.

4. A thief will steal these Jeeps.

5. Feed the seal meat and a pea.

6. Read these brief deals.

7. Eve, do you see a seed?

8. The vet will heal the pet's heel.

9. Keep Steve on the team, Zeke.

10. The beam is seen by the wet team.

Short and Long e

Read the rows across. Listen for the difference between the **short e** sound and the **long e** sound:

bet / beat	pet / Pete
set / seat	Ben / bean
dell / deal	fell / feel
hell / heal	Jen / jean
led / lead	men / mean
Ned / need	red / read
tell / teal	Ted / team
wet / weak	sell / seal
bed / bead	met / meet
peck / peek	pep / peep

Long e – Read for Speed

Read the paragraph below, and have your teacher count the seconds. Write your time in the blank below.

Try to read it in **30 seconds**! If you can't read in 30 seconds, read two more times, and write your times on the blanks below.

> Pete bet Ted that he will make the tennis team. Ted feels that Ted will make the team.
>
> "You are lean and you can leap well," said Ted. "You can make the team!"
>
> "I feel so glad!" said Pete. "If I make the team, will you come to my tennis meet?"
>
> "It's a deal!" said Ted.

Time 1: _____

Time 2: _____

Time 3: _____

Long e vs. Short i

Long e is similar to **short i.** Practice saying the pairs of words below, and try to hear the difference.

bit / beat	bean / bin
sin / seen	ream / rim
dill / deal	seat / sit
pit / Pete	seem / sim
rid / read	keep / Kip
mitt / meat	lean / Lin
lick / leak	peel / pill
riff / reef	deep / dip
pick / peek	reek / Rick
lick / leak	seep / sip
Tim / team	seek / sick
fit / feet	beef / Biff
this / these	meek / Mick

Long e vs. Short i

Numbers Game

Rules (see introduction for more ways to play this game):
- Choose one student to say a word (any word) from below.
- The first student to **find the word** and **say the number** in the box gets to say the next word.

1 Biff	2 deep	3 lick	4 this	5 seen
6 fit	7 leak	8 Tim	9 bet	10 riff
11 read	12 Ron	13 beef	14 keep	15 win
16 sin	17 dip	18 wean	19 feet	20 rid
21 team	22 seek	23 these	24 reef	25 sick

Long e
Homophones

Homophones are words that sound the same, but are spelled differently.

- meat and meet **are homophones**
- heal and heel **are homophones**
- raise and raze **are homophones**

These are homophones because <u>they sound **exactly the same**</u>.

*Remember: Listen to the sound; don't just look at the letters.

Look at the pairs of words below. Write **H** if the words are homophones. Write **R** if the words are rhyming words.

1. bate – bait _____

2. Pete – peat _____

3. bean – mean _____

4. real – reel _____

5. meet – seat _____

6. fee – see _____

7. week – weak _____

8. beat – Pete _____

9. meek – seek _____

10. Gail – gale _____

11. beam – meme _____

12. beat – beet _____

Write a **rhyming word** in each blank.

pin _____   reel _____

seek _____   bum _____

read _____   deep_____

dip _____   bit _____

fat _____   heat _____

team _____   hick _____

Pete _____   feel _____

seat _____   hot _____

Short e vs. Short i vs. Long e

Review

Listen to the words your teacher says, and write **e**, **i**, or **ee** in the blanks below. (Answer key in the back of the book.)

1. s_____ll

2. s_____k

3. p_____k

4. p_____ck

5. t_____n

6. t_____n

7. r_____d

8. r_____d

9. r_____d

10. t_____m

11. T_____m

12. w_____d

13. d_____m

14. w_____k

15. d_____p

16. y_____ll

17. b_____t

18. b_____t

19. b_____t

20. w_____n

Long e

Review Quiz

Write the words and sentences that your teacher says on the blanks below. (Answer key in the back of the book.)

Part 1 – Words (6 points each)

1. _____

2. _____

3. _____

4. _____

5. _____

6. _____

7. _____

8. _____

9. _____

10. _____

Part 2 – Sentences (20 points each)

1. _____.

2. _____.

*See page 52 for more 'long e' reading practice.

1. time	mine	night	hike
2. might	lie	bite	nine
3. tile	fight	dime	file
4. tie	vine	right	size
5. hive	quite	mile	ripe
6. side	tide	die	sight
7. fine	five	hide	bile
8. light	tike	line	file
9. Mike	wide	mime	tight
10. rise	bike	wine	live

Long i

Sentences

1. We can hike a mile at night.

2. That nice dog might bite.

3. The dime is mine but the tie is not mine.

4. Pete and Jay got five mice and a pup.

5. We might like five lights for a dime.

6. The wide mile is right for Mike.

7. The mime has sight and he is fine.

8. The bee in the hive will bite and die.

9. Mike might rise at nine.

10. The tide will rise and get quite high.

Short and Long i

Read the rows across. Listen for the difference between the **short i** and **long i** sounds.

bit / bite	kit / kite
fin / fine	Bill / bile
rip / ripe	mitt / might
sit / site	hid / hide
dim / dime	pip / pipe
lit / light	rid / ride
quit / quite	Tim / time
pick / pike	fit / fight
Mick / Mike	lick / like

Short i and Long i
Review Worksheet

Is it **short i** or **long i**?
Listen to the words your teacher says, and write **"short"** or **"long"** on the blanks below. (Answer key in the back of the book.)

1. _____
2. _____
3. _____
4. _____
5. _____

6. _____
7. _____
8. _____
9. _____
10. _____

Write the words your teacher says below.

1. _____
2. _____
3. _____

4. _____
5. _____
6. _____

Short i and Long i - BINGO

- Write **one word** from **page 23** in each square below.
- When your teacher says a word, write an **X** on the word if you see it in a square.
- The first person to have **5 X's** in a row is the winner!

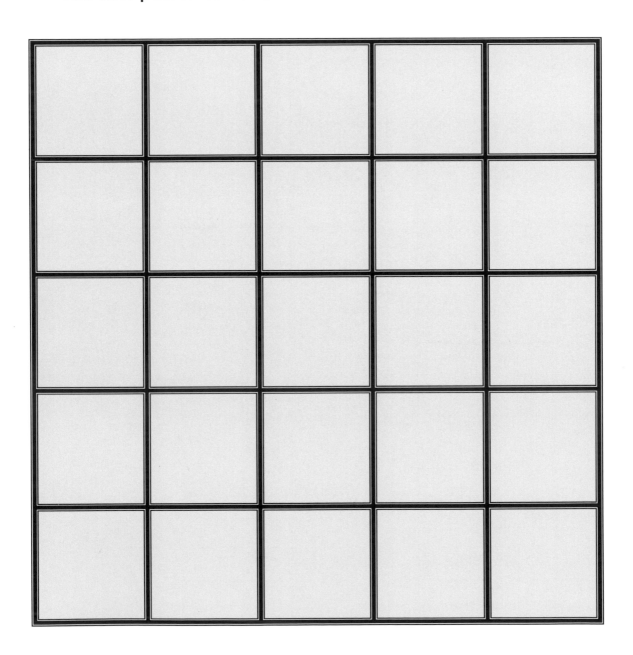

Practice reading these tongue twisters!

1. Kick Kip, keep Kip's kin.

2. Lead lid, lead led deal.

3. Fix Mike's kite, feed Meg's hen.

4. Pick six beaks, seek big peeks.

5. Mick's men met Mike's team.

6. She sells sea shells by the <u>seashore</u>.

Short i, Short e, Long e

Practice saying the groups of words below.

bit bet beat	bean Ben bin
pin pen peen	read red rid
dill dell deal	seat set sit
rid red read	seek seck sick
pit pet Pete	peek peck pick
mitt met meat	need Ned nid
lick leck leak	peat pet pit
riff ref reef	beef beff Biff
pick peck peek	reed red rid
fid fed feed	weed wed wid

Long i

Review Quiz

Write the words and sentences that your teacher says on the blanks below. (Answer key in the back of the book.)

Part 1 – Words (6 points each)

1. _____   6. _____

2. _____   7. _____

3. _____   8. _____

4. _____   9. _____

5. _____   10. _____

Part 2 – Sentences (20 points each)

1. _____.

2. _____.

*See page 53 for more 'long i' reading practice.

1. hope	boat	nose	foam
2. moan	mope	tow	toad
3. soak	load	lone	no
4. go	bow	nope	pole
5. coal	quote	roam	Rome
6. Joan	toe	so	tone
7. vote	low	bone	mode
8. cone	coat	bowl	home
9. note	dome	yoke	foal
10. dote	loan	mow	Joe

Long o

Sentences

1. I hope the boat floats.

2. Joan votes in Rome.

 3. We run home at night and sleep.

4. He can make a bowl with coal and foam.

5. Joe will loan the foal to Joan.

6. The foal will moan when it is alone.

7. Go home and soak a load.

8. Joan will quote Joe's note.

 9. I hope Joan will go to Rome.

10. Nope! I won't throw the toad!

Both **oa** and **o_e** have the same sound.

Look at the words below. Many of them are spelled wrong.
If the word has oa, rewrite it using o_e.
If the word has o_e, rewrite it using oa.

Example:
fome __*foam*__   *doam* __*dome*__

1. bote _____
2. toam _____
3. load _____
4. soke _____
5. joak _____
6. cote _____
7. zoan _____
8. boad _____
9. fome _____
10. gote _____

11. poak _____
12. loan _____
13. hoap _____
14. mone _____
15. noap _____
16. rode _____
17. tode _____
18. quoat _____
19. roap _____
20. woak _____

Long o – Fill in the Blanks

Write one of the words below in each blank to complete the sentences. Then read the sentences out loud.

coat	hope	low	boat
go	toe	road	Joe

1. Joe will _____ to school.

2. It is cold. I will take my _____.

3. Dad likes to drive on the _____.

4. This chair is too _____!

5. There is a _____ on the lake.

6. Oh no! There is a bug on my _____!

7. I think that Joan likes _____.

8. I _____ I can pass the test.

Short and Long o

Read the rows across. Listen for the difference between the **short o** and **long o** sounds.

bot / boat	cod / code
dot / dote	sop / soap
got / goat	hop / hope
jock / joke	lob / lobe
mop / mope	nod / node
cot / coat	Jon / Joan
rod / road	Todd / toad
rot / rote	sock / soak
pock / poke	Ross / rose
cop / cope	Dom / dome

Short and Long o – Sentences

1. The cod will soak in the pot.

2. Ross will poke Dom with a mop.

3. The cop can cope with the road.

4. I <u>know</u> Todd's joke by rote.

5. Joan's coat is on the cot.

6. The jock rode home with Jon.

7. Don can not cope with a hot goat.

8. Nod if you got a note from Ross.

9. Nope! I will not vote for a hot dome.

10. Mop the boat with soap.

Long o – Rhyming Words

Write a **rhyming word** in each blank.

pot _____   rode _____

tome _____   soak _____

con _____   mope _____

rock _____   mob _____

goat _____   low _____

cone _____   pod _____

log _____   cope _____

Ron _____   woe _____

sop _____   Joan _____

Long o – Read for Speed

Read the paragraph below, and have your teacher count the seconds. Write your time in the blank below.

Try to read it in **30 seconds**! If you can't read in 30 seconds, read two more times, and write your times on the blanks below.

> Jon rides a foal to his home, but the foal is slow, so Jon kicks it with his toe. The foal is sick, so the foal will mope and go slow. John will not moan.
>
> "The foal will go slow," says John. "The foal likes to roam and mope. I will let the foal go slow. I will not kick the foal with my toe."

Time 1: _____

Time 2: _____

Time 3: _____

Long o

Numbers Game

Rules (see introduction for more ways to play this game):
- Choose one student to say a word (any word) from below.
- The first student to **find the word** and **say the number** in the box gets to say the next word.

1 dock	2 poke	3 lame	4 mill	5 foam
6 sod	7 vet	8 wine	9 mow	10 rock
11 sight	12 Ron	13 win	14 reek	15 rake
16 sin	17 dub	18 cope	19 sob	20 rid
21 lob	22 take	23 bod	24 bode	25 lobe

Review Quiz

Write the words and sentences that your teacher says on the blanks below. (Answer key in the back of the book.)

Part 1 – Words (6 points each)

1. _____

2. _____

3. _____

4. _____

5. _____

6. _____

7. _____

8. _____

9. _____

10. _____

Part 2 – Sentences (20 points each)

1. _____.

2. _____.

*See page 54 for more 'long o' reading practice.

Long u (*u-e, oo, ew*)

Word List

"oo" sound

1. flew	moon	new	tube
2. lude	dune	cool	boot
3. Sue	toon	noon	blue
4. tune	soon	June	zoo
5. blew	clue	too	rule
6. toot	goose	food	lewd

"you" sound

7. cube	cue	cute	cure
8. mule	mute	muse	puke
9. fume	fuse	fuel	<u>huge</u>

Long u

Sentences

1. The new zoo is too cool.

2. The blue goose flew to the moon.

3. Jon and Rick knew a cute cat.

 4. Meg is cute but she is too rude.

5. The new rule is: No Lewd Tunes.

6. Sue and June are too cool for school.

7. The mute mule is quite cute.

8. The jet flew with no fuel.

9. The huge goose is in the zoo.

10. I need a new clue.

Long u

Both **oo** and **ew** have the same sound.
Write **oo** or **ew** in the blanks below to complete the sentences.
(Look at page 39 if you need help.)

1. The ship fl_____ to the m_____n.

2. The g_____se is so cute!

3. The l_____d lad will t_____t.

4. John has two n_____ b_____ts.

5. Sue kn_____ the clue, t_____.

6. This June is very c_____l.

7. S_____n it will be n_____n.

8. Your n_____ b_____ts are c_____l!

Long u

Tongue Twisters

Practice reading these tongue twisters!

1. New moon, blue moon, new blue moon.

2. Lude Luke knew new tunes.

3. Cute mule, mute mule, cute mute mule.

4. Cute Sue boot blue tube.

5. June knew Sue's blue dune.

6. Fuse fume, muse fume, muse fuse fume.

Short and Long u

Read the rows across. Listen for the difference between the **short u** and **long u** sounds.

cub / cube	bun / boon
dun / dune	sun / soon
cut / cute	rub / rube
Jud / Jude	tub / tube
mutt / mute	duck / duke
luck / Luke	mud / mood
run / rune	nut / newt
Russ / ruse	fuss / fuse
bun / boon	but / boot
dud / dude	ruff / roof

Short and Long u - Sentences

1. The sun will soon rise.

2. Jude is in a bad mood.

3. The ruse is not cute, Russ.

4. My mutt is mute, but it is cute.

5. The newt will run to the rune.

6. The cute cub will fuss and fuss.

7. Luke has bad luck.

8. The duke's duck runs in the dune.

9. Jud and Jude cut a bun on the roof.

10. The cube will melt in the tub.

Short u and Long u

BINGO

- Write **one word** from page 43 in each square below.
- When your teacher says a word, write an **X** on the word if you see it in a square.
- The first person to have **5 X's** in a row is the winner!

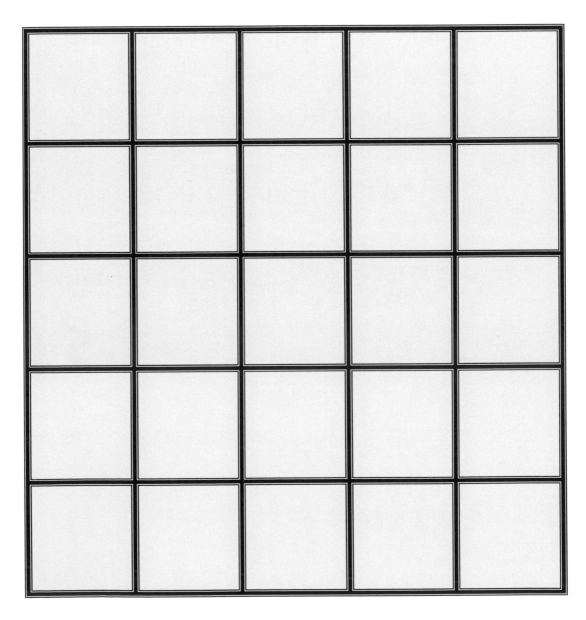

Long u

Review Quiz

Write the words and sentences that your teacher says on the blanks below. (Answer key in the back of the book.)

Part 1 – Words (6 points each)

1. _____   6. _____

2. _____   7. _____

3. _____   8. _____

4. _____   9. _____

5. _____   10. _____

Part 2 – Sentences (20 points each)

1. _____.

2. _____.

*See page 55 for more 'long u' reading practice.

Read the rows across. Listen for the difference between the **short** and **long** vowel sounds.

hat / hate	Dan / Dane
bet / beat	fell / feel
bit / bite	hick / hike
got / goat	hop / hope
tub / tube	cut / cute
gab / Gabe	pan / pain
set / seat	peck / peek
Tim / time	kit / kite
Dom / dome	sop / soap
Russ / ruse	sun / soon

Review – Short and Long Vowels

Sentences

1. He can make a hat with coal and foam.

2. Steve and Pete will not eat red meat.

3. The dime is mine but the tie is not mine.

4. Jed cut the cake and ate a big bite.

 5. Meg is cute but she is very rude.

6. Dale bet Jon that it will rain in five weeks.

 7. The black tube is not mine.

8. I hope the boat will float.

9. Can you make three cakes and then eat them?

Long Vowels

Review Quiz 1

Write the words and sentences that your teacher says on the blanks below. (Answer key in the back of the book.)

Part 1 – Words (6 points each)

1. _____

2. _____

3. _____

4. _____

5. _____

6. _____

7. _____

8. _____

9. _____

10. _____

Part 2 – Sentences (20 points each)

1. _____.

2. _____.

Long Vowels
Review Quiz 2

Write the words and sentences that your teacher says on the blanks below. (Answer key in the back of the book.)

Part 1 – Words (6 points each)

1. _____   6. _____

2. _____   7. _____

3. _____   8. _____

4. _____   9. _____

5. _____   10. _____

Part 2 – Sentences (20 points each)

1. _____.

2. _____.

50

Fay and Jane like to play at the lake. One day, they made a maze in the hay. On the same day, they had rain and hail, so Fay and Jane ran back to play games.

"Can Fay stay and play games?" Jane <u>asked</u> her Dad.

"Fay can stay and play if her mom and dad say it is okay," <u>said</u> Jane's dad.

Fay and Jane <u>stayed</u> up late and <u>played</u> games.

Steve had his pet monkey, Eve, in his jeep. Eve is keen on books, so Steve gave Eve a book to read.

"I need to jog," said Steve. "You can sit in the tree and read, Eve. My jog will be quick."

Eve <u>looked</u> at Steve, and Steve ran on the beach. "I can not read," said Eve. "I will lick the book."

Long i – Reading

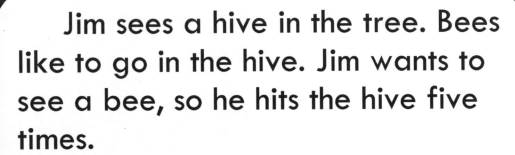

Jim likes to ride his bike and hide by the lake. Today, he rides his bike five miles and stops to rest.

Jim sees a hive in the tree. Bees like to go in the hive. Jim wants to see a bee, so he hits the hive five times.

Six bees fly and see Jim.

"Oh, no!" says Jim.

He runs to his bike, but he can not quite get away. The bees are quite mad. Jim yells and cries and hides.

Jim will not hit the hive five times next time. He will just ride his bike and go away.

Ross likes Joan, so he tells her jokes. Joan does not smile at the jokes. "Woe is me," moans Ross. "I have no hope. I will be alone, with no Joan."

Hope is not lost. Joan has a note for Ross. Ross reads the note. It says, "I like your joke, Ross. Let's go on a date on a boat."

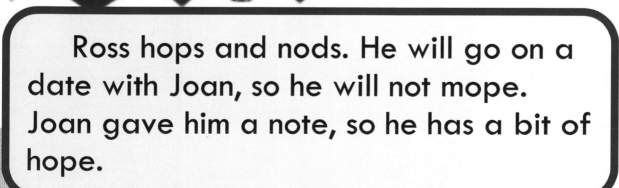

Ross hops and nods. He will go on a date with Joan, so he will not mope. Joan gave him a note, so he has a bit of hope.

Jud has a juke box in his room. Luke likes to play with the juke box, but he will not pay.

"My juke box is not free," he says. "If you want tunes, you must pay."

"But I am your bud," says Luke. "Must I pay to play a tune?"

"Yes, you must," says Jud. "My tunes are good. If you want cool tunes, you must pay <u>first</u>."

"You are too rude," says Luke. "I will listen to tunes at home."

"Wait, wait!" says Jud. "You can stay! The tunes are free! I don't mean to be rude. I am just poor!"

Answer Key

Page 10
Part 1 – Words
1. cape
2. mail
3. bay
4. sake
5. rat
6. pain
7. sack
8. maze
9. rail
10. may

Part 2 – Sentences
1. Jay and Ray hate the game.
2. Pack the bag and take the bait.

Page 19
1. sill
2. seek
3. peek
4. peck
5. teen
6. ten
7. rid
8. red
9. reed
10. teem
11. Tim
12. wed
13. deem
14. week
15. dip
16. yell
17. beet
18. bit
19. bet
20. win

Page 20
Part 1 – Words
1. team
2. teen
3. feel
4. beat (beet)
5. pick
6. Pete
7. seed
8. meek
9. read
10. rid

Part 2 – Sentences
1. We need to see the team
2. Feed the seal beef and a pea.

Page 24
Short/Long
1. pike
2. pick
3. mitt
4. night
5. wide
6. lip
7. like
8. pin
9. dill
10. dine
Words
1. pine
2. fin
3. lit
4. dime
5. wide
6. kid

Page 28
Part 1 – Words
1. night
2. mine
3. fit
4. kite
5. site (sight)
6. bite
7. bit
8. ripe
9. hide
10. rip
Part 2 - Sentences
1. We can hike a mile at night.
2. The nice dog might bite.

Page 38
Part 1 – Words
1. low
2. boat
3. soak
4. dome
5. sock
6. nose (knows)
7. road (rode)
8. boss
9. note
10. hope
Part 2 – Sentences
1. Go home and soak a load.
2. Ross will poke Dom with a mop.

Page 46
Part 1 – Words
1. cube
2. sun
3. boot
4. new (knew)
5. dune
6. rude
7. bud
8. Luke
9. luck
10. toon (tune)
Part 2 – Sentences
1. Meg is cute but she is too rude.
2. Jude is in a bad mood.

Page 49 - Quiz 1
Part 1 – Words
1. make
2. seem (seam)
3. fine
4. load
5. tube
6. moan
7. team
8. Luke
9. same
10. line
Part 2 – Sentences
1. Mike made a fine boat.
2. Rose has a cute cape on the bed.

Page 50 - Quiz 2
Part 1 – Words
1. boot
2. vibe
3. bait
4. seek
5. pine
6. cube
7. vote
8. cape
9. bone
10. feed

Part 2 – Sentences
1. Gabe and Joe will peek at the time.
2. Mike has seen a rude goat.

CPSIA information can be obtained at www.ICGtesting.com
Printed in the USA
LVIW01n1354110816
499993LV00005B/13

*9 7 8 1 4 4 1 4 7 9 4 1 9 *